WORKBOOK
for
Speaking With The Heart

Transforming Your Relationship and Communication with Compassion and Connection: A Guide To Dr. Heather Browne's Book

WILLOW READS

Copyright © 2024 by Willow Reads.

All rights reserved. No part of this workbook may be reproduced, distributed, or transmitted in any form or by any means, including photocopying, recording, or other electronic or mechanical methods, without the prior written permission of the publisher, except in the case of brief quotations embodied in critical reviews and certain other noncommercial uses permitted by copyright law.

Disclaimer!!!

This book is a companion book designed for informational and educational purposes only. The content is based on the ideas presented in the main book but it is not endorsed or affiliated with the author or publisher of the main book.

The workbook is intended to complement and enhance the main book, offering readers additional tools for personal growth and self-reflection. However, the workbook should not be considered a substitute for professional advice, diagnosis, or treatment.

While every effort has been made to ensure the accuracy and completeness of the information in this workbook, the publisher and author assume no responsibility for errors, inaccuracies, or omissions.

About The Author

Willow Reads Workbook Team, we are a distinguished brand of technical authors and literary connoisseurs, with an eye for crafting insightful companion guides for a diverse range of published books. With passion for enhancing readers' experiences, we delve deeply into each book and create workbooks that maximize the information in the original book and help you put it to use practically.

These guides, published by our team, are well researched and connect you out readers more deeply with your favorite books.

Each guide is a testament to the team's dedication to literature and commitment to enriching the reading experience for book lovers around the world.

This book belongs to
_____
_____
_____

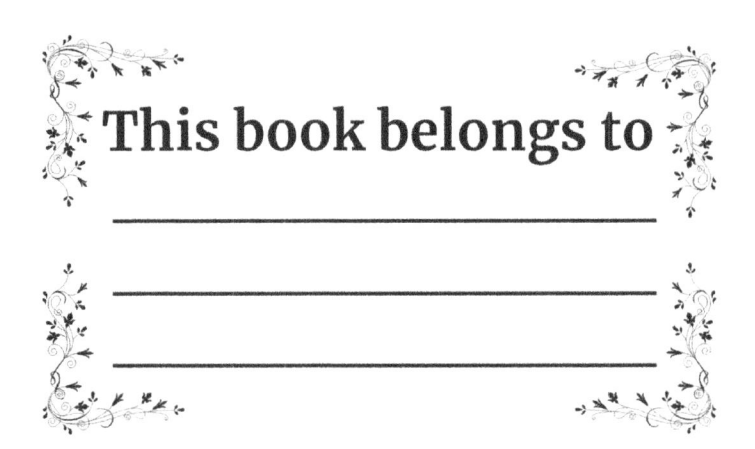

Maximizing The Use Of This Workbook

This workbook is designed to help you engage with the content of the original book in a meaningful and interactive way.

1. Start with the Overview
Begin your journey through this workbook by reading the "Overview of the Original Book." This section provides a concise summary of the key themes and concepts explored in the main book. It's the perfect starting point to refresh your memory or get acquainted with the book's content.

2. Dive into the Chapters
Each chapter in this workbook is dedicated to a corresponding chapter in the original book. Here's what you'll find in each chapter section:

Exercises:
Engage actively with the material through exercises that encourage reflection, application, and critical thinking. These exercises will help you internalize and apply the book's teachings.

Questions:
Explore thought-provoking questions related to the chapter's content. Use these questions for personal

reflection or as a basis for discussions with others who have read the original book.

3. Final Evaluation Questions

Towards the end of this workbook, you'll find a section titled "Final Evaluation Questions." This is your opportunity to test your knowledge and insights gained from the entire book. These questions will challenge you to think critically, make connections, and draw your own conclusions.

4. Your Journey, Your Pace

This workbook is designed to be flexible. You can use it in a way that suits your needs and preferences. Whether you want to complete it in a linear fashion, jump to specific chapters, or revisit sections for further reflection, it's entirely up to you.

Table Of Contents

Overview Of The Original Book............................8
Part 1..10
    Summary... 10
    Key Lessons... 11
    Connection Building Challenge....................12
    Vulnerability Mapping..................................15
    Self-reflection questions............................. 18
    Action Points...22
Part 2..24
    Summary... 24
    Key Lessons... 25
    Self-reflection questions............................. 25
    Action Points...29
Part 3..30
    Summary... 30
    Key Lessons... 31
    Communication Checklist........................... 32
    Self-reflection questions............................. 34
    Action Points...37
Part 4..40
    Summary... 40
    Key Lessons... 41
    Self-reflection questions............................. 41
    Action Points...45

Overview Of The Original Book

This book emphasizes the importance of understanding ourselves and others, practicing empathy, and communicating with authenticity and vulnerability.

Part 1: The Power of Heartfelt Communication
This section lays the foundation for the rest of the book by exploring the concept of heartfelt communication. Dr. Browne defines it as "a way of connecting with others from the deepest parts of ourselves, with genuineness, empathy, and a desire to understand and be understood." She discusses the benefits of heartfelt communication, such as stronger relationships, greater intimacy, and reduced conflict.

Part 2: Understanding Yourself and Others
In this part, Dr. Browne emphasizes the importance of self-awareness and understanding. She discusses the different aspects of our emotional lives, such as our needs, values, and triggers. She also explores the concept of emotional intelligence and how it can help us to better understand and manage our emotions. Additionally, she provides guidance on understanding the perspectives and emotions of others.

Part 3: The Skills of Heartfelt Communication
This section provides practical tools and techniques for communicating with compassion and connection. Dr. Browne covers topics such as active listening, nonviolent communication, and setting boundaries. She also offers guidance on how to express difficult emotions in a healthy way and how to navigate conflict constructively.

Part 4: Putting It All Together

In the final part of the book, Dr. Browne provides guidance on how to apply the principles of heartfelt communication in all areas of your life. She offers tips for improving your relationships with your partner, family, friends, and colleagues. She also discusses how to use heartfelt communication to create a more peaceful and fulfilling life.

Part 1: The Power of Heartfelt Communication

Summary

Part 1 lays the foundation for the entire book by establishing its core: genuine connection through authenticity and vulnerability.

Key Concepts:
1. Shifting the Paradigm: Dr. Browne emphasizes a move away from transactional, ego-driven communication towards a heart-centered approach. This involves connecting with empathy, compassion, and a desire to understand and be understood.

2. Vulnerability as Strength: The book challenges the societal conditioning that equates vulnerability with weakness. Instead, it portrays it as a strength that fosters trust, intimacy, and deeper connections. By sharing true thoughts and feelings, we invite others to reciprocate, creating a space for genuine exchange.

3. Benefits of Heartfelt Communication: The potential benefits are numerous. This approach can strengthen relationships, improve conflict resolution, reduce loneliness, and cultivate overall well-being. The emphasis is on creating a more fulfilling and meaningful life through authentic communication.

4. The Tools of Empathy: Part 1 provides practical tools to put heartfelt communication into action. Active listening, nonviolent communication, and setting healthy boundaries are explored as skills crucial for building deeper connections. The focus is on understanding the emotional landscape of oneself and others, leading to more effective communication.

Key Lessons

1. Heartfelt communication isn't flowery speeches, it's sharing your authentic truth - fears, dreams, and all. This vulnerability may feel risky, but it builds trust and intimacy, the bedrock of strong relationships.

2. Seek to understand the emotions and needs behind actions, both yours and the other person's. This empathy paves the way for constructive communication and conflict resolution.

Connection Building Challenge

Challenge 1: Share Your Story
- Objective: Initiate a genuine conversation by sharing a personal experience with someone.

Instructions:
1. Choose a personal story or moment that shaped you.
2. Find a suitable time to share this story with a friend, family member, or colleague.
3. Pay attention to their response and be open to further discussion.

How did it feel to share your story?

_____

_____

What insights did you gain from their response?

_____

_____

Did this exchange deepen your connection with the other person?

_____

_____

Challenge 2: Express Gratitude
- Objective: Strengthen connections by expressing gratitude to someone in your life.

Instructions:
1. Identify someone you appreciate and want to thank.
2. Write a heartfelt note expressing your gratitude.
3. Choose a method (letter, email, in person) to deliver your message.

How did the act of expressing gratitude impact your relationship?

_____

_____

_____

_____

Did it create a positive shift in the dynamic between you and the other person?

_____

_____

_____

Challenge 3: Walk in Their Shoes
- Objective: Understand someone else's perspective by actively listening and seeking to empathize.

Instructions:
1. Choose a person with whom you have a varying viewpoint.
2. Initiate a conversation with the intention of understanding their perspective.
3. Practice active listening without judgment.

What did you learn about their perspective that you didn't know before?

_____

_____

_____

How did this exercise contribute to a more empathetic connection?

_____

_____

_____

Vulnerability Mapping

Objective:

Identify areas of your life where you can embrace vulnerability. Promote self-awareness and a commitment to personal and professional growth through openness.

Reflection on Perceived Strengths and Weaknesses

Instructions:

1. Reflect on your perceived strengths and weaknesses in both personal and professional aspects of your life.
2. Identify situations where you tend to avoid vulnerability due to perceived weaknesses.
3. Consider how embracing vulnerability in these situations could lead to personal growth.

How do you perceive vulnerability in relation to your strengths and weaknesses?

_____

_____

_____

_____

In which areas of your life do you typically avoid being vulnerable?

_____

_____

_____

_____

Identifying Areas for Vulnerability

Instructions:

1. Create a map or list of personal and professional aspects of your life.

2. Mark or highlight areas where you recognize the potential for increased vulnerability.

3. Consider specific actions or changes that embody vulnerability in these identified areas.

What specific situations or aspects have you identified as areas for vulnerability?

_____

_____

_____

How might embracing vulnerability in these areas contribute to personal and professional development?

_____

_____

Commitment to Vulnerability

Instructions:
1. Write a personal commitment statement to embrace vulnerability in the identified areas.
2. Specify actionable steps you can take to embody vulnerability in your daily life.
3. Share your commitment statement with a trusted friend, family member, or colleague for accountability.

What actionable steps can you take to practice vulnerability in the identified areas?

_____

_____

_____

How do you anticipate your commitment to vulnerability will impact your personal and professional life?

_____

_____

_____

_____

Self-reflection questions

When was the last time you shared a raw, unfiltered truth with someone, even if it made you feel vulnerable? Did the connection deepen as a result?

_____

_____

_____

_____

_____

_____

Replay a recent disagreement you had. Are there moments where you could have chosen empathy instead of blame, understanding instead of judgment? How might that have shifted the conversation?

_____

_____

_____

_____

_____

_____

_____

Think of someone you struggle to communicate with. What assumptions do you hold about them that might be blocking deeper connection? What questions could you ask to bridge the gap?

_____

_____

_____

_____

_____

_____

Notice your typical reaction to difficult emotions in conversations. Do you bottle them up, lash out, or try to fix things for others? Can you identify a healthier way to express your needs and feelings?

_____
_____
_____
_____
_____
_____
_____
_____

Are there parts of yourself you keep hidden away, fearing rejection or misunderstanding? Can you imagine taking a small step toward sharing one of these hidden pieces with someone you trust?

_____
_____
_____
_____

_____
_____
_____
_____

Picture your ideal relationship: strong, intimate, and supportive. What specific actions and choices can you make, starting today, to move your current connections closer to that vision?

_____
_____
_____
_____
_____
_____
_____

Action Points

1. Practice non-judgmental listening: Instead of interrupting or formulating your response while the other person talks, focus on truly hearing them. Make eye contact, nod subtly, and ask clarifying questions that show you're engaged. Try this next time a friend vents or your partner shares a concern.

2. Start small with vulnerability: Begin by sharing a less charged emotion or experience. Acknowledge a fear before making a request, or express gratitude for something your partner did. Notice how this "micro-vulnerability" affects the conversation and build upon it over time.

Part 2: Understanding Yourself and Others

Summary

This section isn't just about introspection; it's a call to develop emotional intelligence, becoming attuned to both your own inner landscape and the intricate emotional worlds of those around you.

Key Concepts:

1. Self-Awareness: Dr. Browne emphasizes the importance of understanding your needs, values, triggers, and emotional patterns. She encourages introspection through various exercises, helping you identify the driving forces behind your thoughts, feelings, and behaviors.

2. Emotional Intelligence: Beyond mere self-awareness, she advocates for developing emotional intelligence (EQ). This encompasses recognizing and managing your own emotions, as well as perceiving and responding effectively to the emotions of others.

3. Compassion: Understanding yourself paves the way for understanding others. Dr. Browne encourages cultivating compassion, a deep empathy for the emotional experiences of others, even when they differ from your own.

4. Perspective-Taking: She emphasizes the importance of stepping outside your own perspective and seeing the world through the eyes of others. This involves considering their background, values, and emotional triggers to interpret their actions and reactions with greater understanding.

Key Lessons

1. Explore your needs, values, and triggers. This self-awareness helps you predict your reactions and make conscious choices, leading to better communication and personal growth.

2. Practice perspective-taking, considering the background, values, and emotions of others. This fosters empathy and allows you to communicate with understanding and compassion, strengthening relationships.

Self-reflection questions

Close your eyes and take a deep breath. What emotion is bubbling just beneath the surface, unacknowledged but influencing your current mood? Can you name it and offer it some understanding?

_____

_____

_____

_____

_____

_____

_____

Picture a recent conflict. Which part of your emotional terrain (needs, values, triggers) got activated? Now, imagine the other person's perspective. What might their emotional map look like in this situation?

_____

_____

_____

_____

_____

_____

_____

_____

Think of someone you find challenging to connect with. What assumptions do you hold about them, their beliefs, or their experiences? How might these assumptions be clouding your ability to truly see and understand them?

_____

_____

_____

_____

_____

_____

_____

Recall a moment when someone listened to you deeply, without judgment or advice. What emotions did this evoke in you? How can you cultivate that quality of attentive listening in your own interactions?

_____

_____

_____

_____

Consider a recurring pattern in your relationships. Do you tend to withdraw, push away, or get defensive when certain emotional buttons are pressed? What alternative, more mindful response could you choose next time?

Imagine your ideal relationship: built on trust, acceptance, and open communication. What specific actions and practices can you implement today to move closer to that ideal, both in your interactions with others and your understanding of yourself?

_____

_____

_____

_____

_____

_____

_____

Action Points

1. Practice "feeling check-ins" with yourself and others: Throughout the day, take a moment to pause and identify your own emotions. Acknowledge them without judgment, and then ask someone close, "How are you feeling right now?" Actively listen to their response without jumping to advice or solutions. This simple practice strengthens both self-awareness and empathy.

2. Start a "curiosity journal" about someone you want to understand better: Jot down observations about their behavior, reactions, and communication style. Ask open-ended questions and actively listen to their answers. Look for

underlying feelings and motivations. This journal becomes a safe space to explore your assumptions and cultivate genuine understanding of the other person.

Part 3: The Skills of Heartfelt Communication

Summary

This section is a toolbox, filled with instruments to navigate the often delicate terrain of human interaction.

Key Concepts:

1. Active Listening: The foundation of any communication exchange, Dr. Browne emphasizes the importance of truly listening, not just waiting for your turn to speak. Paying attention to verbal and nonverbal cues, asking clarifying questions, and seeking understanding are key aspects of active listening.

2. Nonviolent Communication (NVC): This framework is presented as a powerful tool for expressing needs and feelings without resorting to blame or judgment. By focusing on observations, feelings, needs, and requests, NVC fosters more constructive and empathetic communication.

3. Setting Healthy Boundaries: Part 3 explores the crucial skill of setting clear and respectful boundaries. This involves identifying your needs and limitations, communicating them assertively, and upholding them without guilt or manipulation. Healthy boundaries protect your emotional well-being and contribute to healthier relationships.

4. Expressing Difficult Emotions: Navigating emotions like anger, sadness, and disappointment can be challenging. The book offers frameworks for expressing these emotions constructively, using "I" statements and focusing on ownership of your feelings without blaming or attacking others.

Key Lessons

1. Ditch the "you did" and "you made me feel" statements. Shift to expressing your feelings and needs ("I feel sad when..." or "I need clarity on..."). This non-blaming approach fosters understanding and constructive dialogue.

2. Set clear limits on what you will and won't accept with assertive, "I"-based communication. Healthy boundaries safeguard your well-being and build trust in relationships.

Communication Checklist

Active Listening:

[ ] Focused Attention: I give my full attention to the speaker without distractions.

[ ] Nonverbal Cues: I use positive body language, such as nodding and maintaining eye contact.

[ ] Clarifying Questions: I ask questions to ensure understanding and demonstrate active engagement.

[ ] Avoiding Interruptions: I refrain from interrupting the speaker and patiently wait for my turn to respond.

Nonviolent Communication (NVC):

[ ] Observations: I focus on describing observable behaviors without judgment.

[ ] Feelings: I express my emotions using "I" statements without blaming others.

[ ] Needs: I communicate my needs clearly and respectfully.

[ ] Requests: I make requests rather than demands, allowing room for negotiation.

Expressing Difficult Emotions:

[ ] Ownership: I take ownership of my emotions without blaming or attacking others.

[ ] "I" Statements: I express my feelings using "I" statements to convey personal experiences.

[ ] Constructive Expression: I communicate difficult emotions in a way that fosters understanding and resolution.

[ ] Empathy: I acknowledge and respond empathetically to others' emotions.

Use this checklist to self-assess your communication skills. Check the items that you feel confident in and identify areas for improvement. Regularly revisit and update to track your progress in enhancing communication.

Self-reflection questions

Recall a recent disagreement. Did you jump to blame or attack, or did you try to understand the other person's perspective using active listening and open-ended questions? How might shifting your approach have changed the outcome?

_____

_____

_____

_____

_____

_____

_____

Think of someone you struggle to communicate with. Are there boundaries you need to set to protect your emotional well-being? How can you do this assertively and respectfully, yet remain open to connection?

_____

_____

_____

_____

_____

_____

_____

Picture a situation where you typically bottle up your emotions. Can you identify the fear or discomfort behind this silence? What small step could you take towards expressing your feelings constructively, using "I" statements and owning your experience?

_____

_____

_____

_____

_____

_____

Replay a conversation where you felt unheard or misunderstood. Were you fully present and actively listening, or were you already formulating your response? How can you cultivate deeper attention and presence in your future interactions?

_____

_____

_____

_____

_____

_____

Consider a recurring communication pattern in your relationships. Do you tend to become critical, withdraw, or shut down when your needs or expectations are unmet? What alternative, more mindful response could you choose next time?

_____

_____

_____

_____

_____

_____

Imagine an ideal conversation with someone you care about. What skills would you want to bring to the table: active listening, clear boundary setting, or expressing difficult emotions openly? How can you start practicing these skills in smaller interactions today?

_____

_____

_____

_____

_____

_____

Action Points

1. Turn "why" into "what" practice: When a conflict arises, resist the urge to ask accusatory "why" questions. Instead, shift to curiosity and understanding by asking open-ended "what" questions. "What happened that led you to feel this

way?" or "What could I have done differently to support you?" This fosters communication based on seeking clarity and finding solutions together.

2. Start small with boundaries: Setting boundaries can feel daunting. Begin with something manageable, like establishing your availability for phone calls or saying "no" to extra commitments. Clearly communicate your needs and limitations using a simple "I" statement: "I appreciate the invitation, but I need to prioritize my rest time in the evenings." Remember, small steps towards healthy boundaries build confidence and contribute to stronger relationships.

Part 4: Putting It All Together

Summary

This section serves as a comprehensive guide for integrating the principles of heartfelt communication into every aspect of your life, weaving them into the very fabric of your relationships and experiences.

Key Concepts:

1. Relationships - From Intimate to Professional: Dr. Browne provides tailored guidance for applying heartfelt communication in diverse relationship spheres. For romantic partners, she emphasizes vulnerability, shared goals, and conflict resolution. With family and friends, authenticity, empathy, and healthy boundaries come to the forefront. In professional settings, respectful communication, clear boundaries, and collaborative problem-solving take center stage.

2. Beyond Words - Embodiment and Presence: The section goes beyond mere spoken words, highlighting the importance of nonverbal communication. Active listening through body language and eye contact, mindfulness to emotional cues, and the power of touch in cultivating deeper connection are explored.

3. Cultivating a Heartfelt Life: Heartfelt communication isn't just a tool for individual interactions; it can permeate your entire approach to life. Dr. Browne encourages readers to

apply empathy and compassion to their interactions with the world around them, fostering a more peaceful and meaningful existence.

Key Lessons

1. Apply the core principles of heartfelt communication (vulnerability, empathy, etc.) to different relationships. With partners, prioritize shared goals and conflict resolution. With family and friends, focus on authenticity and healthy boundaries. In professional settings, cultivate respectful communication and collaboration.

2. Nonverbal cues like eye contact and active listening play a crucial role. Be mindful of emotional signals and utilize the power of touch to strengthen connections. This presence elevates your communication on a deeper level.

Self-reflection questions

Think of a relationship that feels stagnant or strained. Could your communication patterns be contributing to this distance? What small step could you take towards vulnerability or empathy to bridge the gap?

_____

_____

_____

_____

Reflect on your work environment. Do you navigate disagreements and challenges with respectful communication and collaboration? How could you prioritize a more empathetic and solution-oriented approach with colleagues?

_____

_____

_____

_____

_____

_____

_____

Recall a recent interaction with a close friend or family member. Did you truly listen to their emotional undercurrents, or were you preoccupied with your own thoughts and responses? How can you cultivate deeper presence and active listening in your future conversations?

___

Picture a personal dream or aspiration. How could applying the principles of heartfelt communication, like authenticity and setting boundaries, empower you to pursue this dream with greater self-belief and support from others?

___

_____

_____

Take stock of your current interactions with the world around you. Do you approach strangers and social situations with warmth and open communication, or do you tend to withdraw or remain guarded? How could integrating empathy and compassion into your daily interactions create a more fulfilling and connected life?

_____

_____

_____

_____

_____

Imagine your ideal life, infused with meaningful connections and inner peace. What specific actions and choices, rooted in heartfelt communication, can you start taking today to move closer to this vision?

_____

_____

_____

_____

_____

_____

Action Points

1. Choose one relationship you want to improve: Select a friend, family member, or colleague where you wish to deepen connection. This week, focus on initiating one small act of heartfelt communication in your interactions. Share a vulnerable truth, practice active listening by asking open-ended questions, or express appreciation for their unique qualities. Observe how this single act creates a shift in the dynamic and use it as a springboard for further connection.

2. Start your "empathy journal": Dedicate a notebook to cultivating daily awareness of the emotions around you. Observe interactions in public spaces, listen to snippets of conversations, or simply reflect on your own emotional state throughout the day. In your journal, try to understand the emotions you perceive, both positive and negative. This practice strengthens your empathy muscle and makes you more attuned to the emotional landscape of yourself and others, both in personal and professional interactions.

Final Evaluation Questions

What did you learn from this workbook that you didn't know before?

_____

_____

_____

_____

_____

How has the information in this workbook impacted your understanding of the subject matter?

_____

_____

_____

_____

Can you identify any areas where you still feel uncertain or would like further clarification?

_____

_____

_____

_____

Describe any challenges you faced while completing the exercises in this workbook and how you overcame them.

_____

_____

_____

_____

How do you plan to apply the knowledge and skills you've gained from this workbook in your work or daily life?

_____

_____

_____

_____

_____

Are there any specific topics or concepts you would like to explore further after completing this workbook?

_____

_____

_____

_____

Overall, how would you rate your learning experience with this workbook on a scale of 1 to 10, with 10 being the highest? Please explain your rating.

_____

_____

Dear reader,

Thank you for choosing this workbook. Your engagement with the content is truly appreciated. As a team, we are committed to continuous improvement and providing valuable insights to our readers.

We kindly request a moment of your time to share your thoughts on the book. Your honest review will not only provide valuable feedback but also assist potential readers in making informed decisions.

Please consider addressing the following points in your review:

What resonated with you the most?
Were the questions and exercises helpful?
How would you describe the overall impact of the book on your understanding or perspective?
Were the chapter summaries effective in reinforcing key concepts?

Your input is instrumental in shaping future projects and ensuring that they meet the expectations of readers like you. Feel free to express your thoughts openly, as your feedback is genuinely valued.

Once again, thank you for your time and consideration. Your support means the world, and we are eager to hear your insights.

Best Regards,
Willow Reads Workbook Team.

Made in the USA
Las Vegas, NV
17 April 2025